GHASTLY PERILS
of the Great Outdoors

GHASTLY PERILS
OF THE GREAT OUTDOORS

by
PETER FARROW

NORTH COUNTRY PRESS
THORNDIKE, MAINE

© 1986 by Peter Farrow. All rights reserved.
Designed by Diane de Grasse
Composition by Type & Design
Printed in United States of America

Library of Congress Cataloging-in-Publication Data

Farrow, Peter.
   Ghastly perils of the great outdoors.

  1. American wit and humor. 2. Outdoor life—
New England—Anecdotes, facetiae, satire, etc.
3. Animals, Mythical—New England—Anecdotes,
facetiae, satire, etc. 4. New England—Anecdotes,
facetiae, satire, etc. 5. Bestiaries. I. Title.
II. Title: Ghastly perils.
PS3556.A7783G4   1986   858'.91402   86-23526
ISBN 0-89621-102-9 (pbk.)

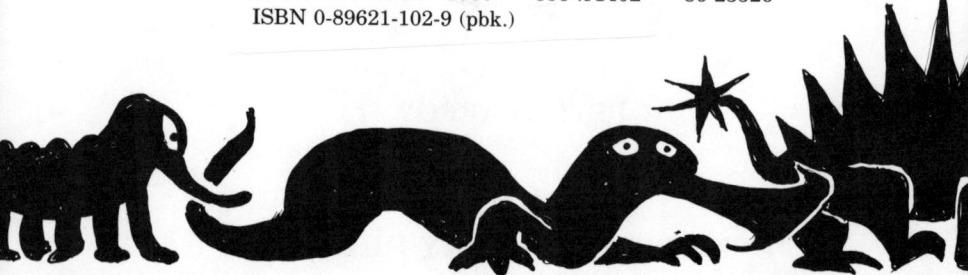

For George and Gwen, who
have bested more Perils than
this or any book can hold.

BE GLAD YOU WEREN'T BORN SOONER...
(A Brief History)

Ghastly as today's Perils may be to the newcomer, they are a far cry from those faced by our Yankee forebears, who either drove them to extinction or reduced them to manageable size. The last *definite* Womkeag, for instance, was reported by its sole survivor in 1934, while the Snowsnake nowadays seldom exceeds 20 feet (except, of course, in its vernal form as the Mud Adder). History's infamous Rumweevil, which once threatened the entire livelihood of New England, is today's miniscule Tipplethrip, not worth our notice here. Even the long-dreaded Puritan Ethic now lurks only in the musty shade of legislatures, pulpits and other last ditches.

But a few of these ancient Perils have left such indelible marks on the New England landscape that they deserve noting, at least briefly.

The Side-Hill Gouger
(Gnashus cianbrosi)

With its flair for the spectacular, no Peril has shaped scenic New England more than the Side-Hill Gouger. New Hampshire's Tuckerman's Ravine, for instance, is the product of a single midmorning snack, while Maine's Mt. Katahdin, to which Mt. Washington was long an insignificant foothill, has been nibbled down to its present pitiful 5,274 feet in less than a century.

Once domesticated by Yankee road builders in the days before dynamite, the public use of the 'Gouger has been banned since the odd (if unlamented) disappearance in 1936 of Fustis Junction, Vermont, the last-known enclave of Democrats in that otherwise flawless state.

Mt. Katahdin before....   Mt. Katahdin after....

The Rockpush
(Petriprofligatus pushuppus)

Contrary to legend, the Rockpush was a welcome helpmate back in the days when Yankees were desperately in need of rocks for their famous stone walls. Indeed, tradition has it that the Rockpush set the standard for New England's endless hospitality: *"Help yourself! There's aplenty more where these come from!"*

Today encountered only as a harmless little garden pest with a wry sense of humor, the Rockpush still continues to be a blessing to a few New England towns.

The Treesqueak
(Squeaccus sylvestrus)

Some of the greatest changes in New England landscape have been caused by some of the smallest Perils, of which the Treesqueak is the prime example.

Lacking vocal chords of its own for its mating rites, its incessant screeking, scraping, scritching and squeaking of treelimbs — a horrifying sound, like fingernails on blackboards — kept much of New England from being permanently settled. Though abated somewhat by the invention of the Maine earmuff, this pestilence was not brought under control till full-time professional eradicators volunteered their services, to which we still owe thanks for much of New England's majestic silence and unimpeded vistas.

TRAVEL PERILS

The Perils of travel are so subtle and disparate that the victim usually passes off misadventures as mere coincidence. Actually, he is ensnared in a complex, well-coordinated *plot,* which begins the moment he stops at his first tollbooth.

The Tollfumble
(Fumblus sequestrus)

This odd little fellow slips into unsuspecting vehicles at turnpike entrances and immediately commences hiding spare change. Though its deftest antics were once reserved for drivers swooping confidently into Exact-Change lanes during rush hours, the Tollfumble has now taken to hiding whole toll tickets. A few, expanding their range from highway to wilderness, specialize in hunting and fishing licenses, duck stamps, fire permits and other critical documents.

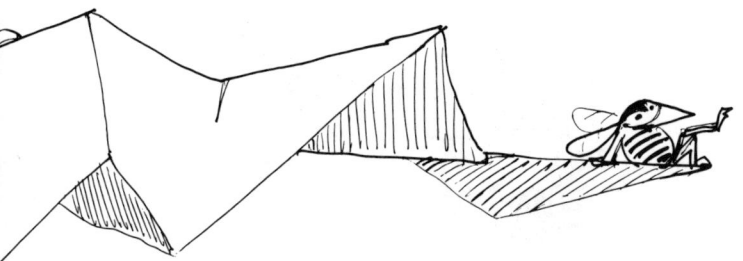

The Mapknit
(Cartofoldium origami)

Attempts to avoid the Tollfumble by using back roads are seldom successful, for these "scenic" routes are the favorite haunt of the Mapknit, who makes it impossible not only to refold roadmaps but to *un*fold them to the right place to begin with. So universal has this Peril become that, to save their customers frustration, gas stations refuse to give out maps at all.

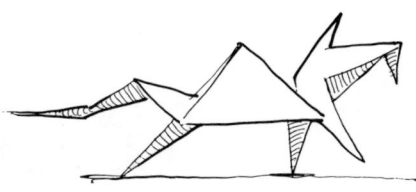

The Bumsteer
(Via disastrum)

The Mapknit is a minor nuisance compared to the Bumsteer. Usually disguised as preternaturally friendly natives, these Perils pop up — always in the nick of time — to assure lost motorists that they *can* get there from here.

Experts on the subject of shortcuts, its family members and near relatives usually operate tow trucks, wreckers, quaint repair shops and even quainter free-lance motels.

Frostheaves
(Crystali collapsum)

A springtime bane (February 15 - June 30) these subterranean Perils construct intricate crystaline structures just below the surface of roads, which collapse under the slightest pressure, revealing — too late — the mud-drenched caverns where dwells the Mud Adder (too ghastly to be depicted or described).

Dormant colonies of Frostheaves can be spotted by the potpourri of hubcaps, mufflers, tailpipes, jacks, planks, blocks — and occasional drivers — which work their way to the surface after Mud Season ends in late July.

The Tarchuck
(Cavitator macadamadora)

In New England, "chuck hole" is no mere figure of speech, and the
                l   them the
              e   t   b
           s   u
              o   e
        s   b
          a   t
   said   t
                                 e
                                  r

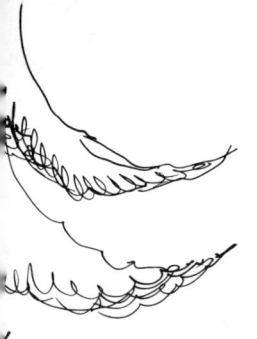

The Rutgrinder
(Terramasticator maximus)

Motorists who would explore the deeper hinterlands of New England will inevitably run afoul of this Peril, which entices them with wide, well-beaten, forest-lined trails that end without warning in sumps, stumptangles and punjipits.

Zealous conservationists, leaping on purely circumstantial evidence, blame innocent loggers and God-fearing pulp companies for the depredations of this monster, which has bested not only Bigfoot but the mighty Subaru itself.

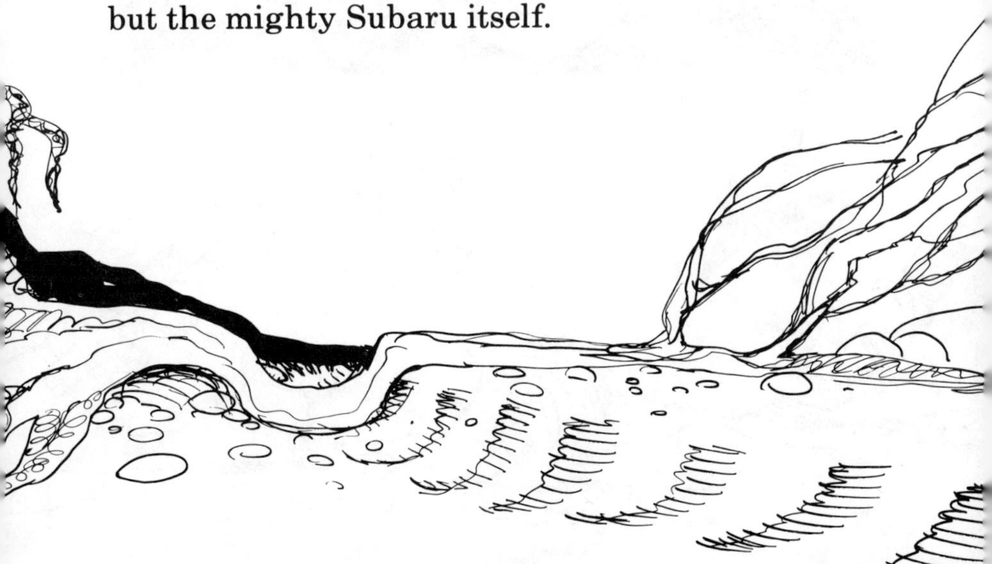

The Bootshuck
(Podinudiator shuccus)

Travelers who despair of wheeled vehicles won't improve their chances by going afoot. They may, however, take some comfort in knowing that the Bootshuck imperils the native no less than the stranger: That odd tined tool carried by clam-diggers is not, as most suppose, used to catch clams (they are nipped up one by one by their little necks). The "clam" hoe is used strictly for retrieving footgear.

HIKING & CAMPING PERILS

The Packroc
(Dorsoagonitum saggapaccus)

These merry little chaps hitch free rides, often adding fifty or more pounds of themselves by the day's end. More nuisance than outright Peril, the *saggapaccus* aids greatly in development of dorsal, pectoral and even gluteal musculature.

The Bootpearl
(Limpus toscanini)

The higher your laces, the more certain the eventual presence of the Bootpearl. Beginning its life cycle as an invisible, unshakeoutable airborne mote, it swiftly accretes itself into a nubby, spiney and often noisome lump, growing as much as an inch in diameter per mile.

The Abominable Sphagnum
(Suncus spongi)

Mistaken by some for the truly formidable Womkeag (p. 7), the *Suncus* rolls out before the traveler's weary feet what *looks* like soft, smooth, lush green carpet — formed, unfortunately, by the tips of its sphagna (feathers) projecting above waist-deep pools of cold and stagnant water.

The Tenttwanger
(Plunccus noctis)

Though a sprinkling of hard-bitten old campers still claim they can ignore the musical propensities of the Tenttwanger, the wise tentsman not only tightens his tentropes but *tunes* them, mindful of both harmonics and resonant frequency. Though C-flat and E-sharp are these little fellows' favorite keys, some may work all night to attain the haunting, rarely-used key of N.

The Pinbeaver
(Gnawum poingum)

The Tenttwanger is not the only Peril facing the tentster. Those diligent little nibbles and gnawings one hears in the night may well be the sounds of the Poingus, or Pinbeaver at work. Positive identification can be made if the noises are followed by a sudden earsplitting *poing* and a state of utter collapse.

MISCELLANEOUS NONINDIGENOUS PERILS

Getting *in* from the Great Outdoors can pose as many Perils as staying out in it. But since few of these Perils are native to New England — most

have been introduced by New Yorkers and other amateurs — we'll give only passing mention here to the *Downsnitch,* the *Zippergrapper* and the *Bumbershoot.* The *Nightlump,* or *Bedroc,* unless confused with the Rockpush (page 11) is soon gotten used to.

The Filtch
(Sequestrus necessitata)

No, you *didn't* forget to pack the canopener. The jackknife *was* safely tucked in your pocket. *And* the compass. And you *did* put the cap back on the fuel can...

A distant relative of the Tollfumble, the Filtch's penchant for larceny forces even experienced outdoorspersons to carry at least two of everything and three of some — a strategy that works almost ten percent of the time.

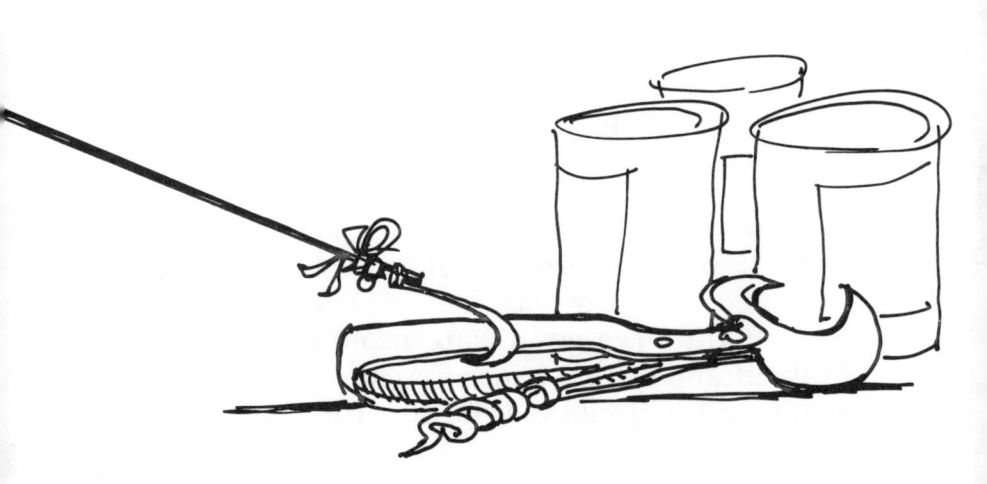

The Matchdamper
(Contraconflagratum coldcampus)

With a ferocity far outstripping even Smokey the Bear, the Matchdamper's vigilance borders on the paranoid. Able to penetrate even paraffined matches hermetically sealed in waterproof containers, the Matchdamper has, on many documented occasions, rendered flickless the infallible Bic itself.

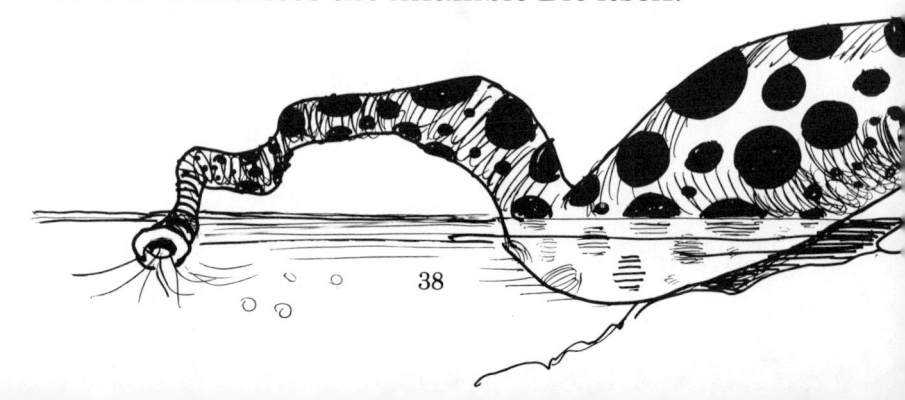

The Canoe Squirt
(Dribblum oozi)

The Canoe Squirt is responsible for that two inches of inexplicable water to be found each morning in the bilges of all watercraft. Never the product of dew, rain, fog, mist, sweat, or other condensates, even craft kept entirely under cover and upside down are not exempt, if not from the 'Squirt outright, then from its relative, the *Lesser Boatbladder (Dribblum incontinenti)* which has been known to breach even the seams of Beanboots.

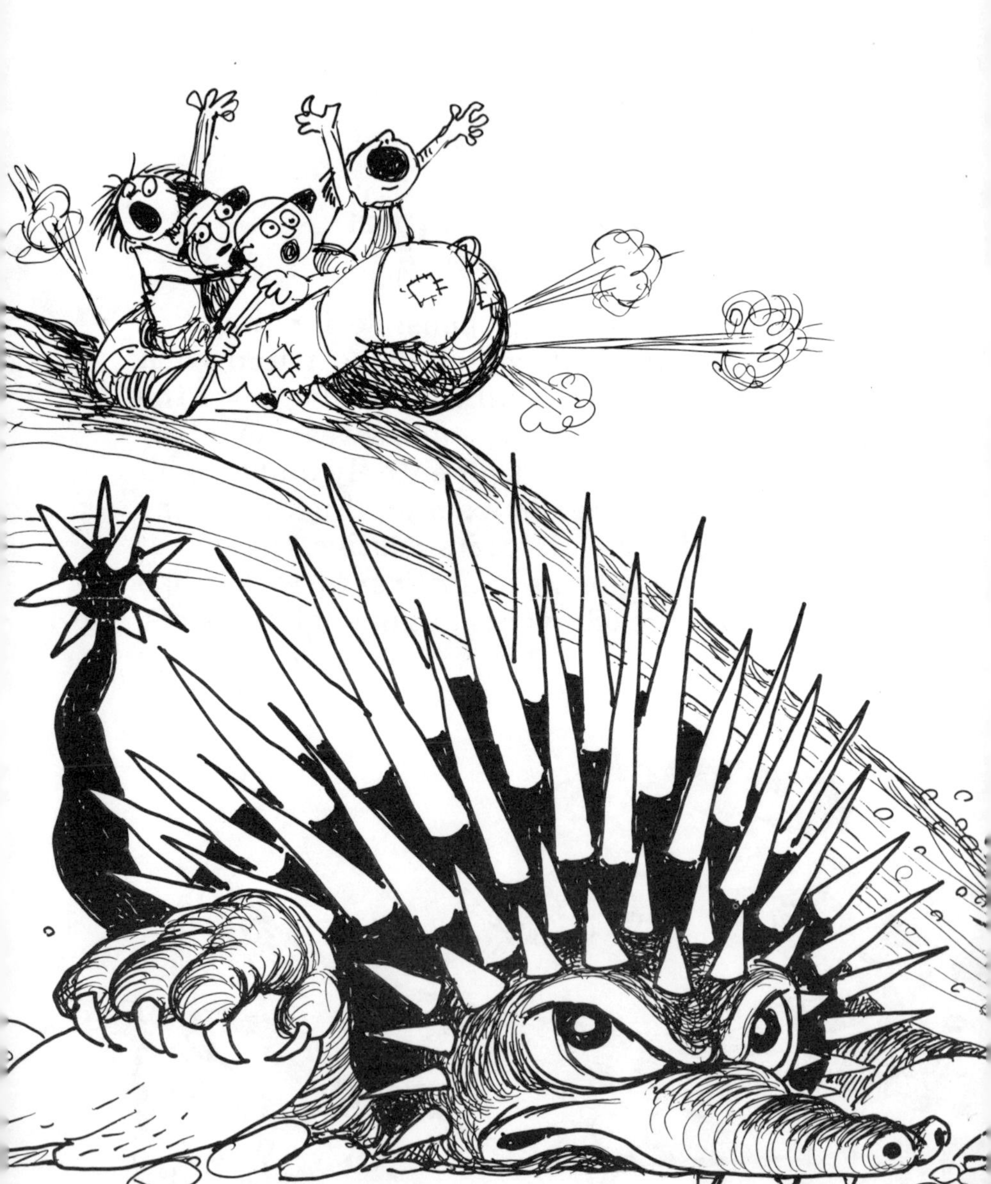

The Whitewater Porcupine
(Pneumopunctus aquablanca)

Though long ago driven from our pristine beaches, where it once wreaked its havoc on the innertubes and waterwings of yesteryear, the *Pneumopunctus* has come into its own again with the introduction of rafting.

Concerned utility and paper companies have offered repeatedly to safeguard the public against this Peril by damming — at their own expense — the more grossly infested streams. Sadly, this corporate altruism has met with little public support. As a result, the ravages of this Peril continue unabated — as the terror-stricken screams of innocent rafters well testify.

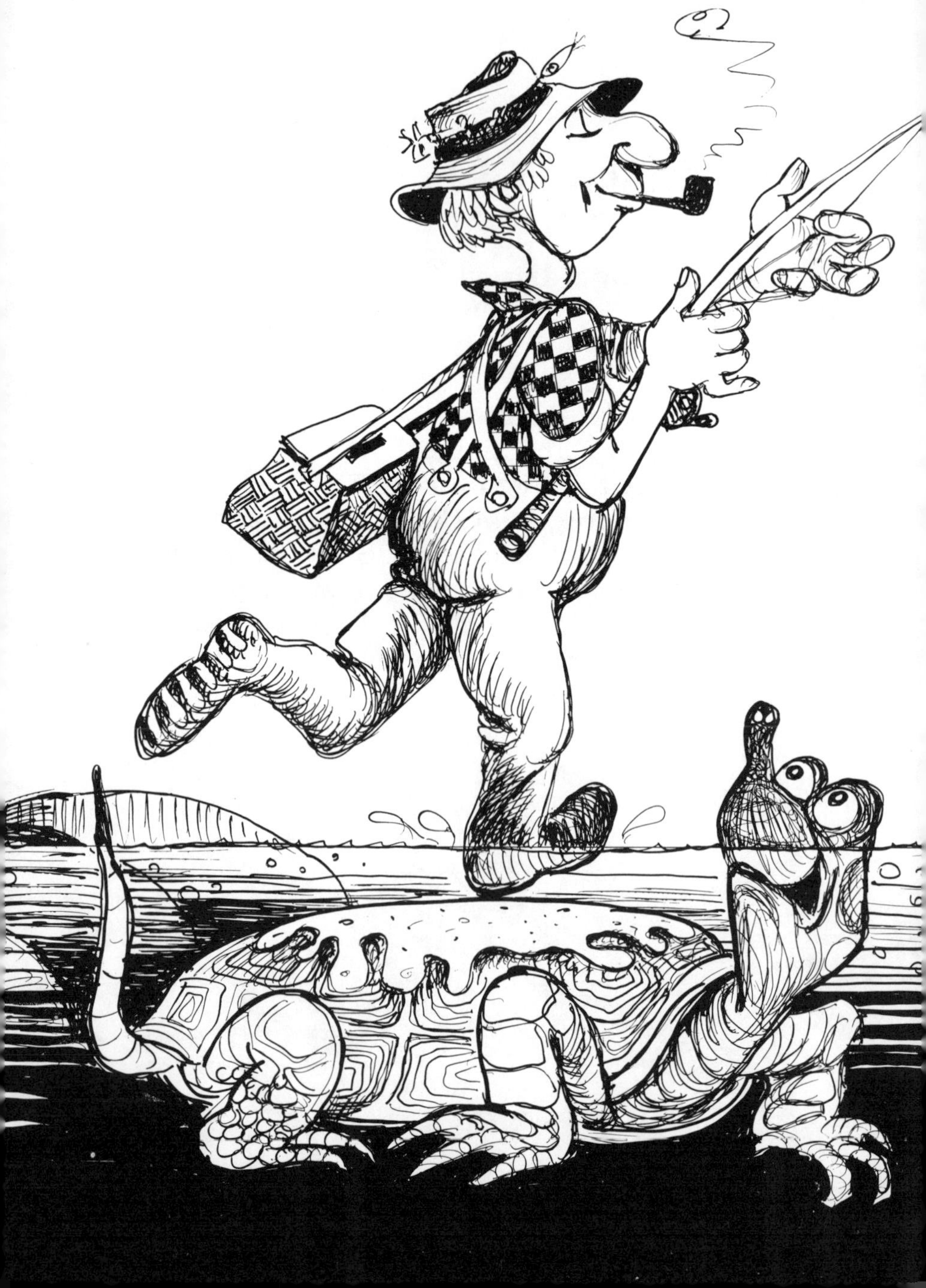

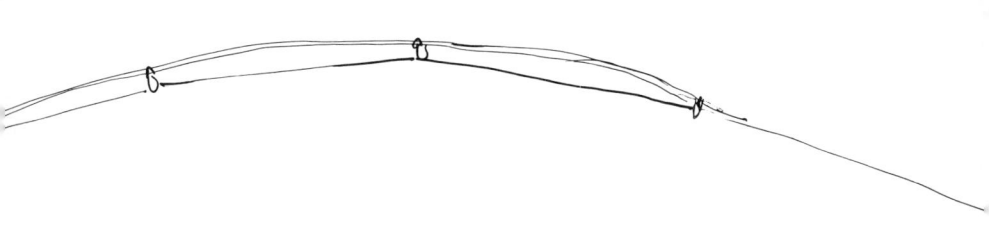

PERILS OF FIELD & STREAM

For some inexplicable reason, Perils demonstrate a powerful penchant for the sportsperson. While massive public relations efforts have eradicated the Horsesnapper, the Creelweevil and even the Blackfly, anglers and hunters should not let themselves be lulled into a false sense of security. Flyfishermen, for instance, will invariably encounter

The Slimeturtle
(Mucosa dunctus)

Craftily camouflaging themselves as large, firm rocks in the beds of trout-burgeoned streams, the *dunctus* instantly exudes a thick, inelegant coating of slime whenever stepped on.

While many public-spirited industries have selflessly contributed H_2SO_4 and other rare and costly effluents in efforts to control this Peril, the Slimeturtle not only survives but flourishes. In many streams fish populations have had to be eradicated entirely to avoid accidents.

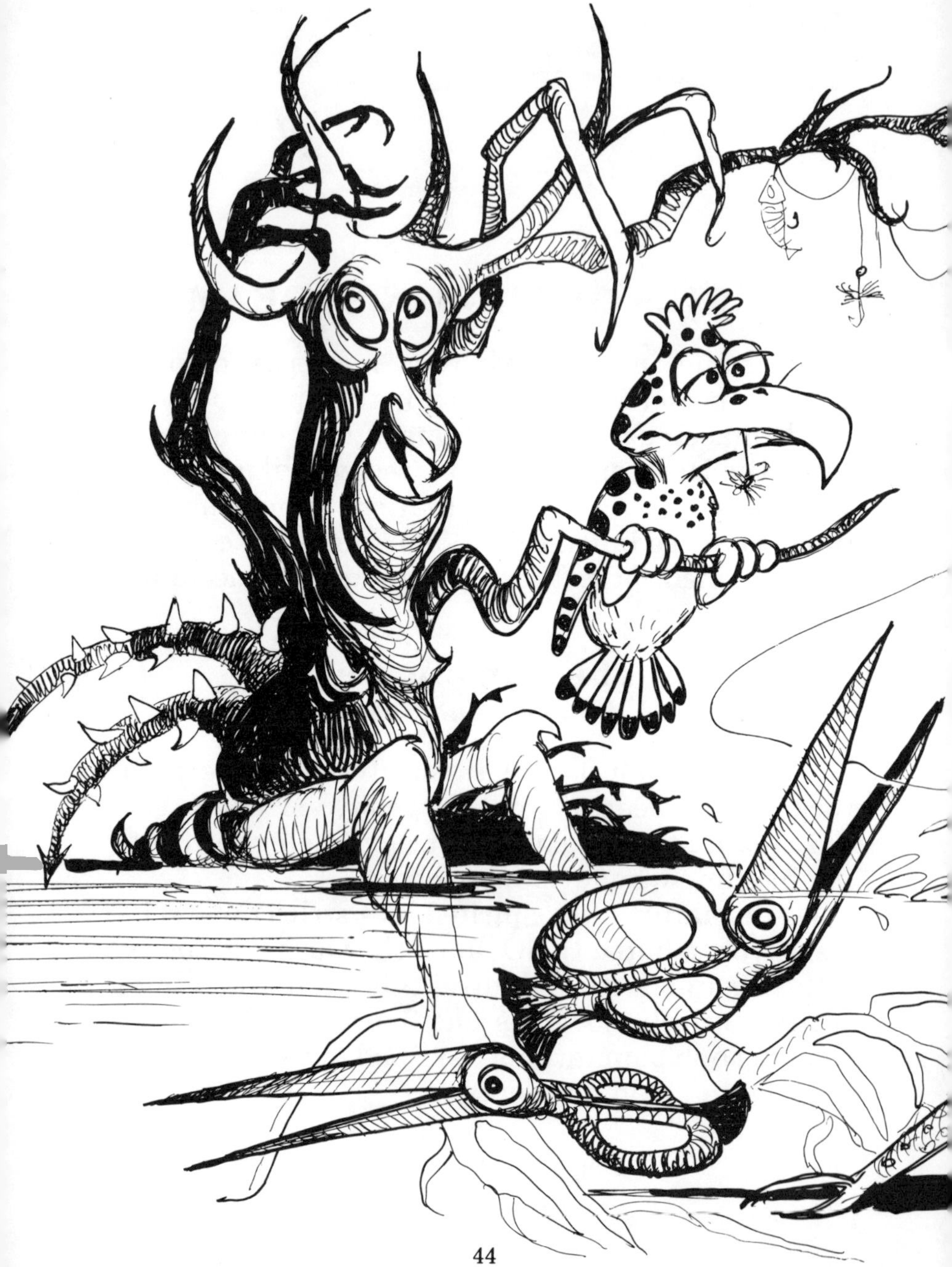

The Luresnags
(Contracastae goddammit)

In or out of water, no Peril in all Nature is more adept in the art of mimicry than the Luresnag, taking on a dozen disguises — roots, stumps, twigs, whole treelimbs, random briarcanes, and even thistles. The flycaster hoping to avoid this Peril may only find himself the victim of the *Shortsighted Flycatcher (Gulpus myopiae)*, and fishermen who do actually succeed in hitting water will, sooner or later, be beset at some critical moment by the *Scissorfish (Snippitus snelli)*.

The hunter fares no better than the fisherman. Take the case of

The Buckfoot
(Pseudopodium buccus)

The larger and more clear the track, the more certain it is to be the work of the Buckfoot. Appearing most frequently in bad terrain and worse weather, it leads the huntsperson on for miles of fruitless tracking.

In Maine, a larger, moose-sized species has recently developed, leading the nimrod not up trees but into bottomless bogs and muskeags.

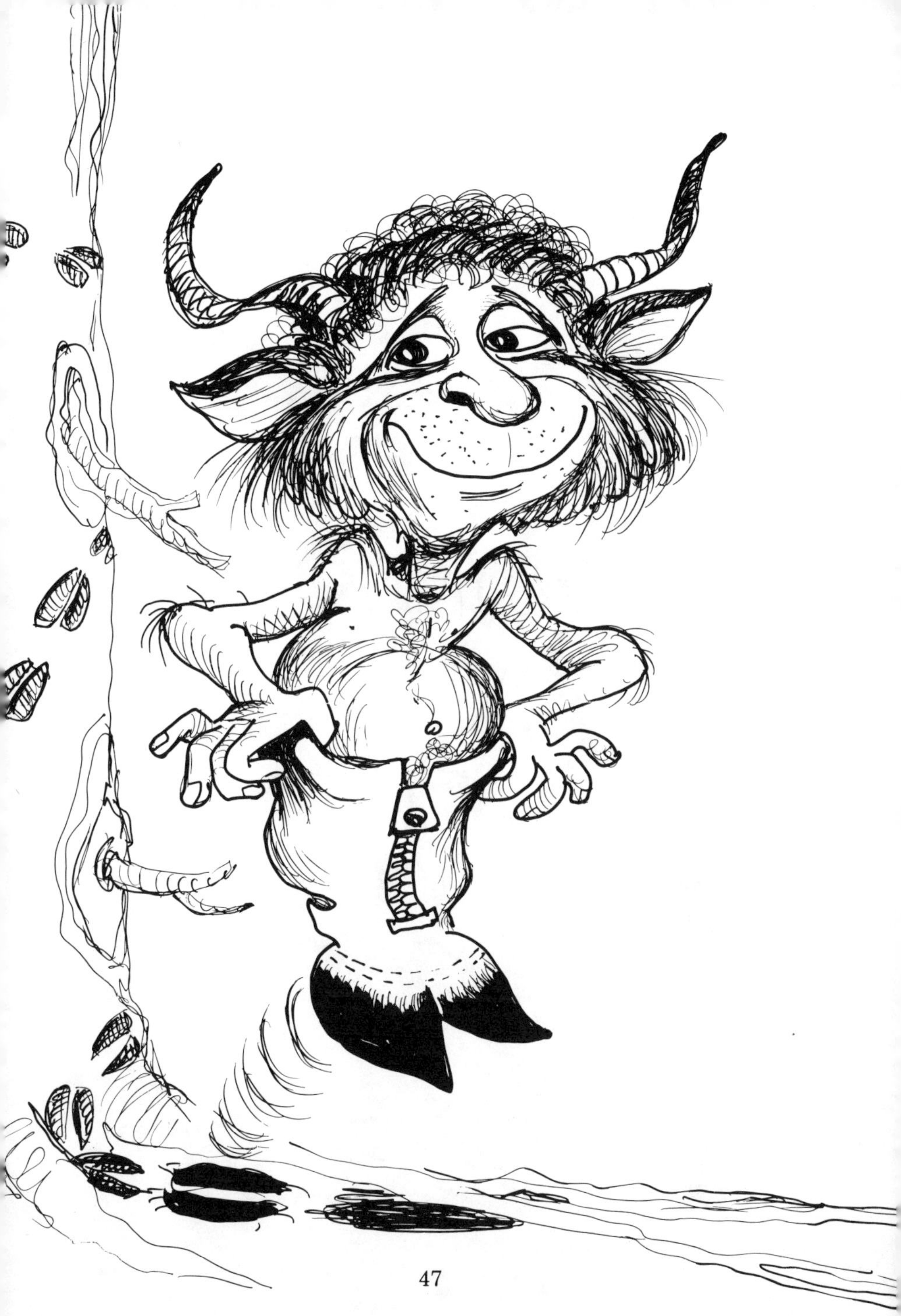

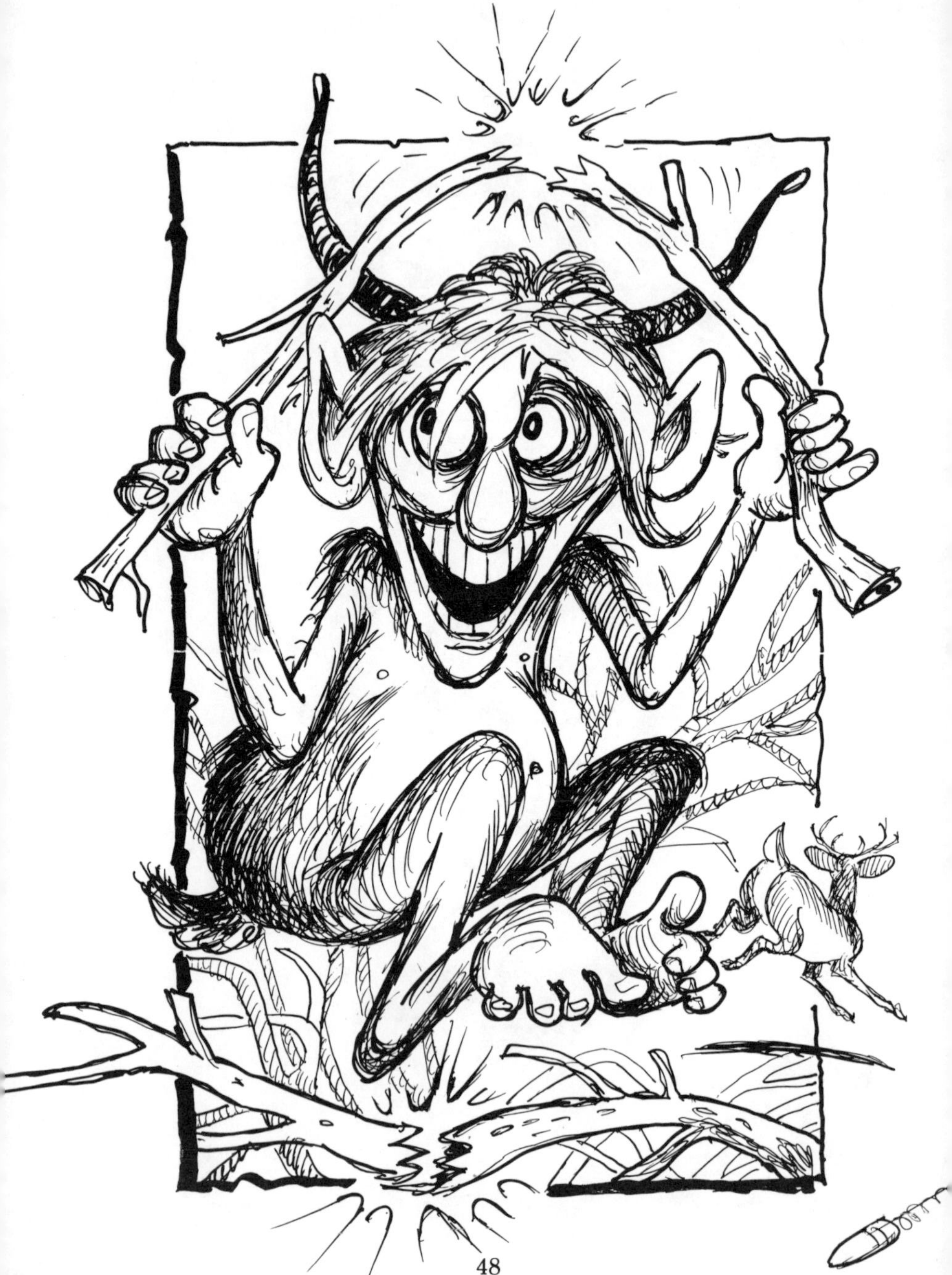

The Twigsnap
(Caveator quarrigone)

Though superficially resembling the Buckfoot, and a possible relative of the Treesqueak, the Twigsnap, instead of leading the hunter, follows close behind, working its barely audible — but wholly sufficient — mischief at the last instant before the hunter gets within range of his quarry.

Though a more passive Peril, one should also beware the *Buckbush (Buccomagnificat possibilis)*, some specimens of which grow as many as fourteen points. While safe enough to shoot at, in no event is it a bush to ever go behind.

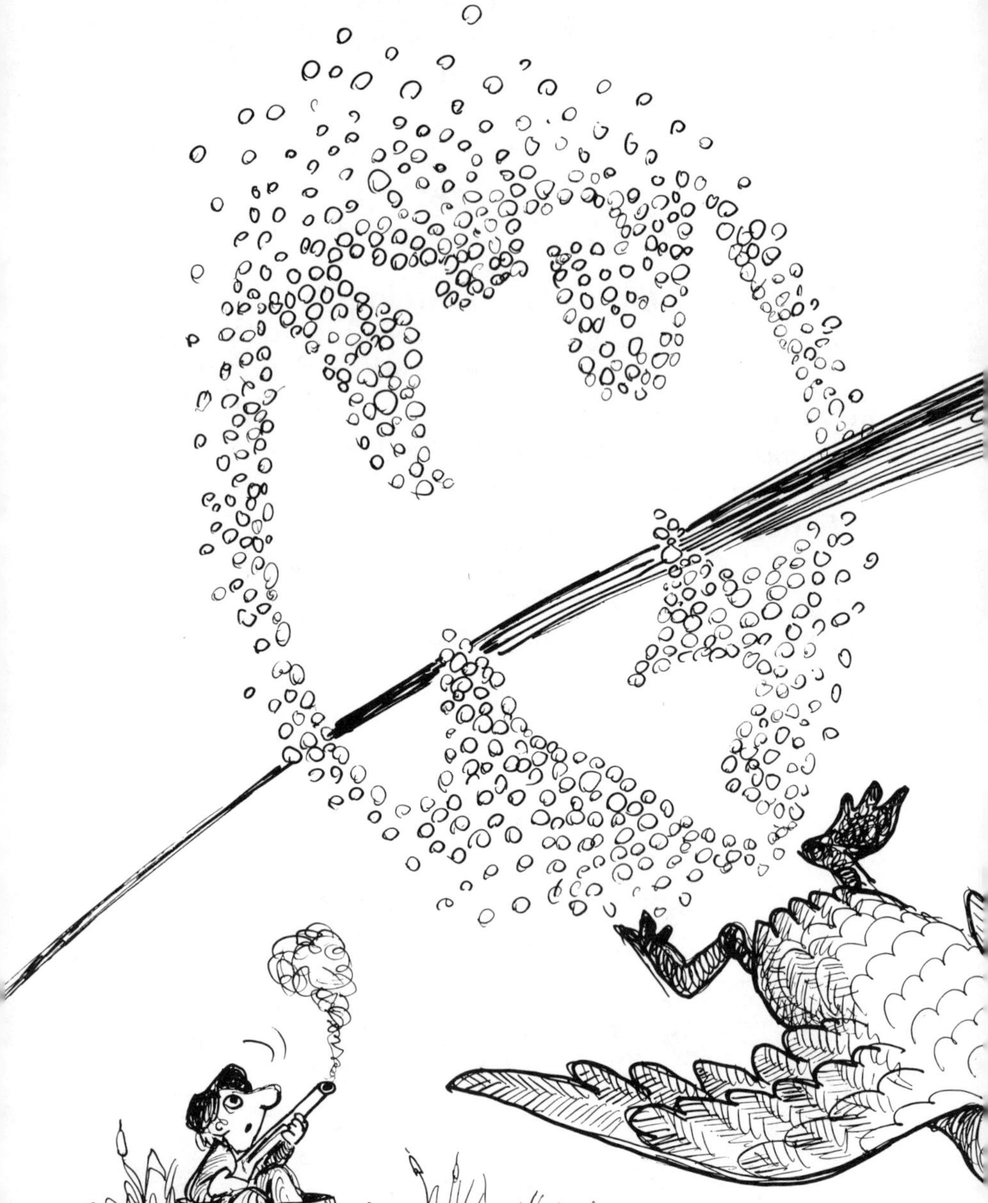

The Shotsucker
(Ingestus pelletae)

The Shotsucker is the exclusive Peril of that oddest of all outdoorspersons, the Duckhunter. By some process, repeatedly verified but by no means understood, the Shotsucker creates peculiar duck-shaped holes in shot patterns in midair.

Off-season, it has been sighted hovering over skeetfields.

The Rustpecker
(Contraziebarti perforatum)

The overnight appearance of rust spots on gun barrels is a certain sign that the discovery has come too late. Traditionally working from the inside out, the Rustpecker spends its larval stage in grooves, lands, bolts, sears, connectors, and other ordnal viscera. Reaching adulthood, it descends in flocks of several thousands, feasting almost exclusively on car metal, though recent studies indicate that it is developing a taste — if not yet quite a preference — for Bondo as well.

LARVAL STAGE (X10)

52

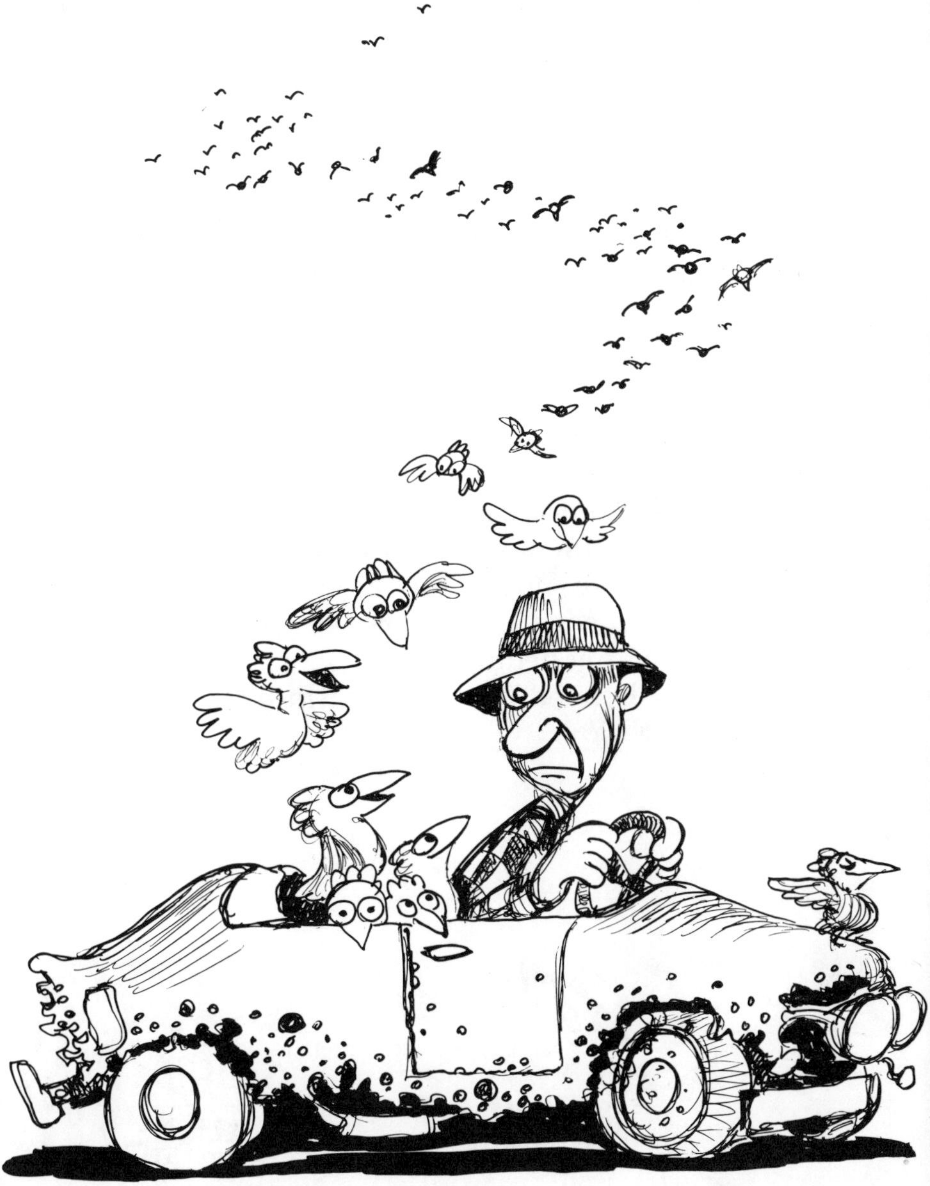

NON-PERILS

It is equally important that the serious outdoorsperson knows what is *not* a Peril.

Weather

For instance, one never need fear a weather shortage. Weather-breeding has been a traditional, highly-skilled profession in New England for centuries. While most of our product is exported, we always reserve enough for our own use and share it without stint with all visitors — even New Yorkers. There is no finer hedge against boredom, monotony, or dull egg-headed "prediction" than New England Weather. Enjoy.

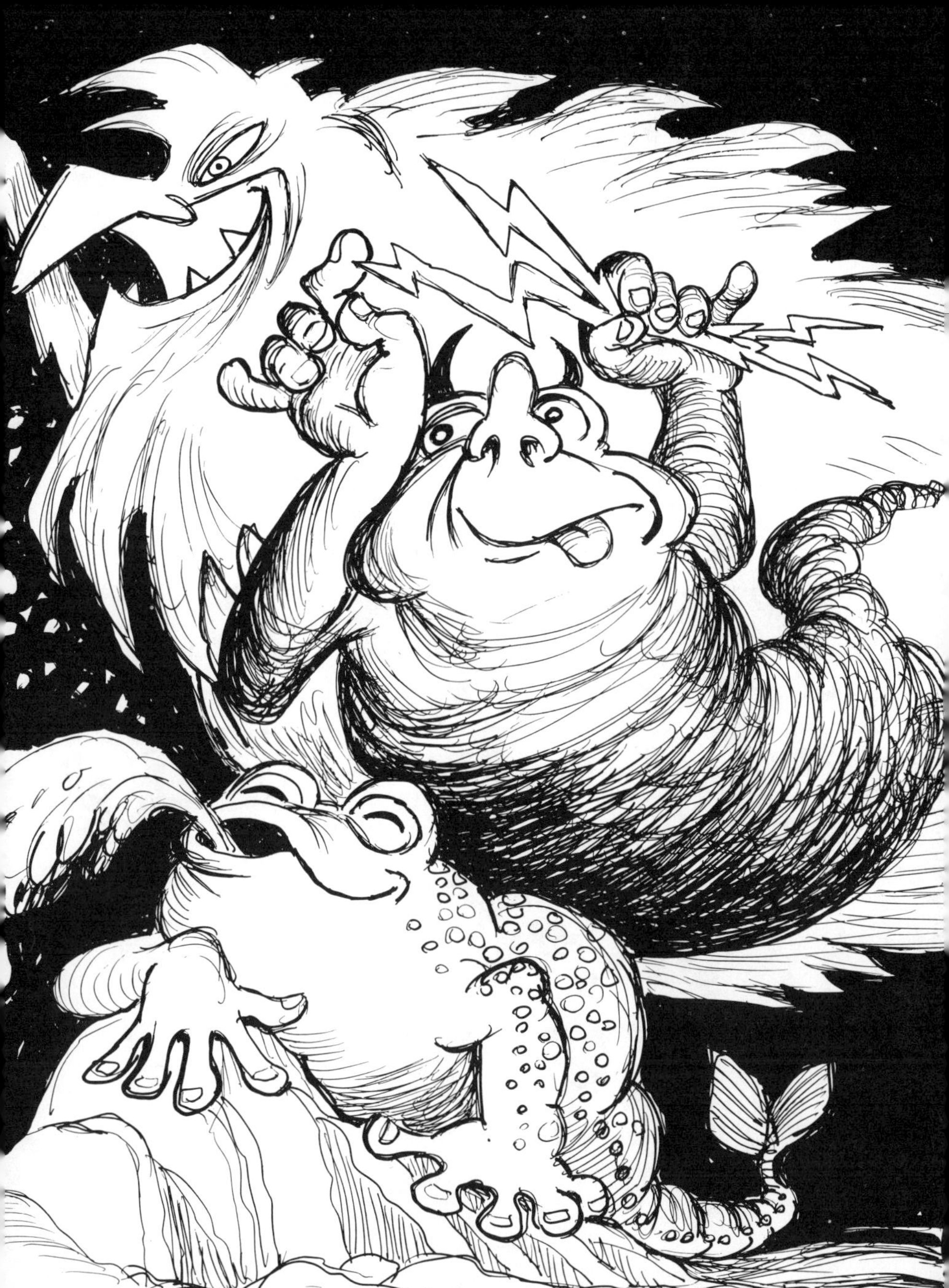

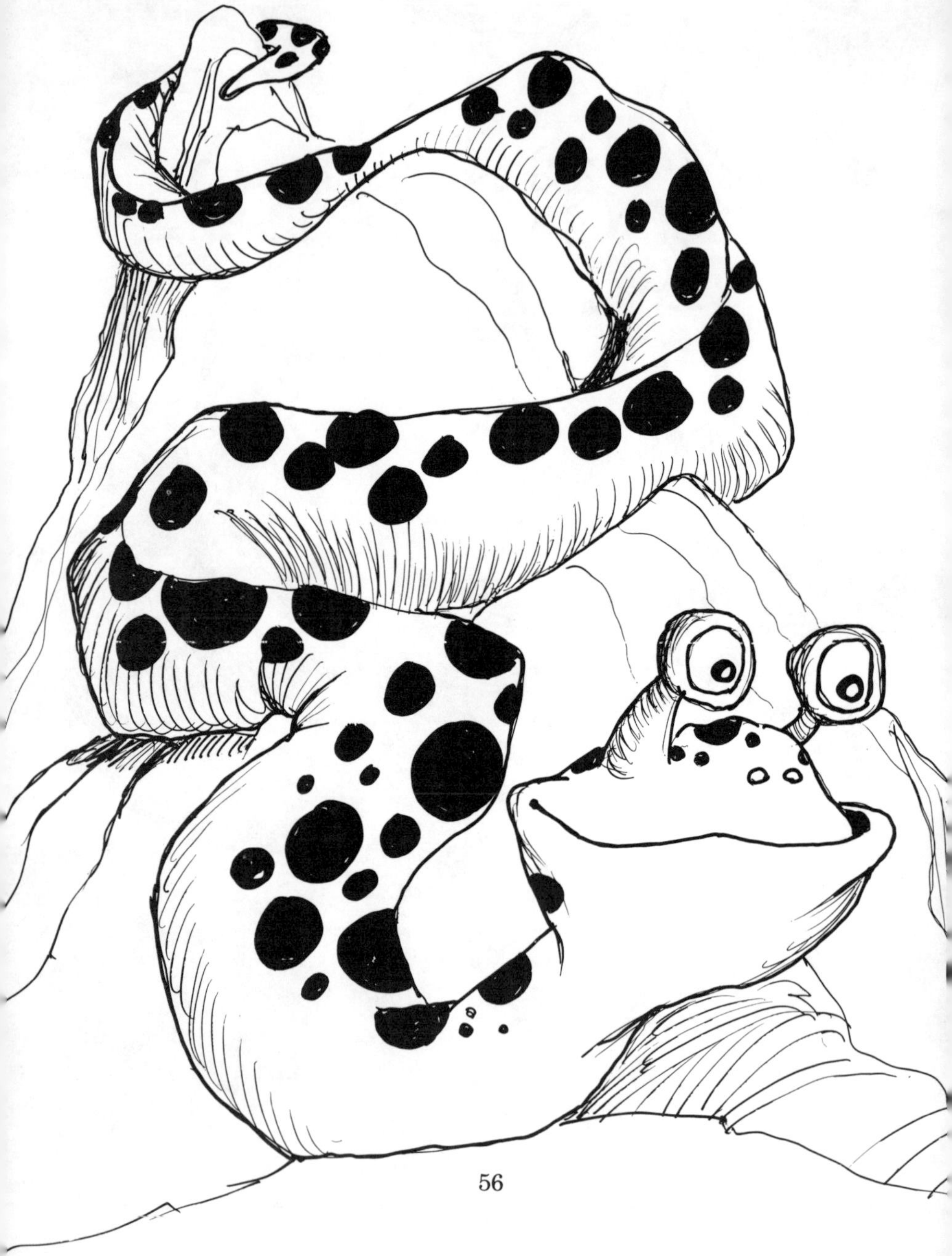

The Snowsnake
or
Downhill Glazer
(Catapultum fractis)

The products of Weather have been libeled as badly as Weather itself. A case in point is the Snowsnake. Repressive, ill-advised legislation has banished it to the hinterlands where, shuffling its unhappy coils on ski slopes, it has become known as the Downhill Glazer. While its hot underbelly does create invisible streaks of shaggy ice, it is otherwise wholly harmless, adding, in fact, a certain primitive, manly zest to this long overcoddled sport.

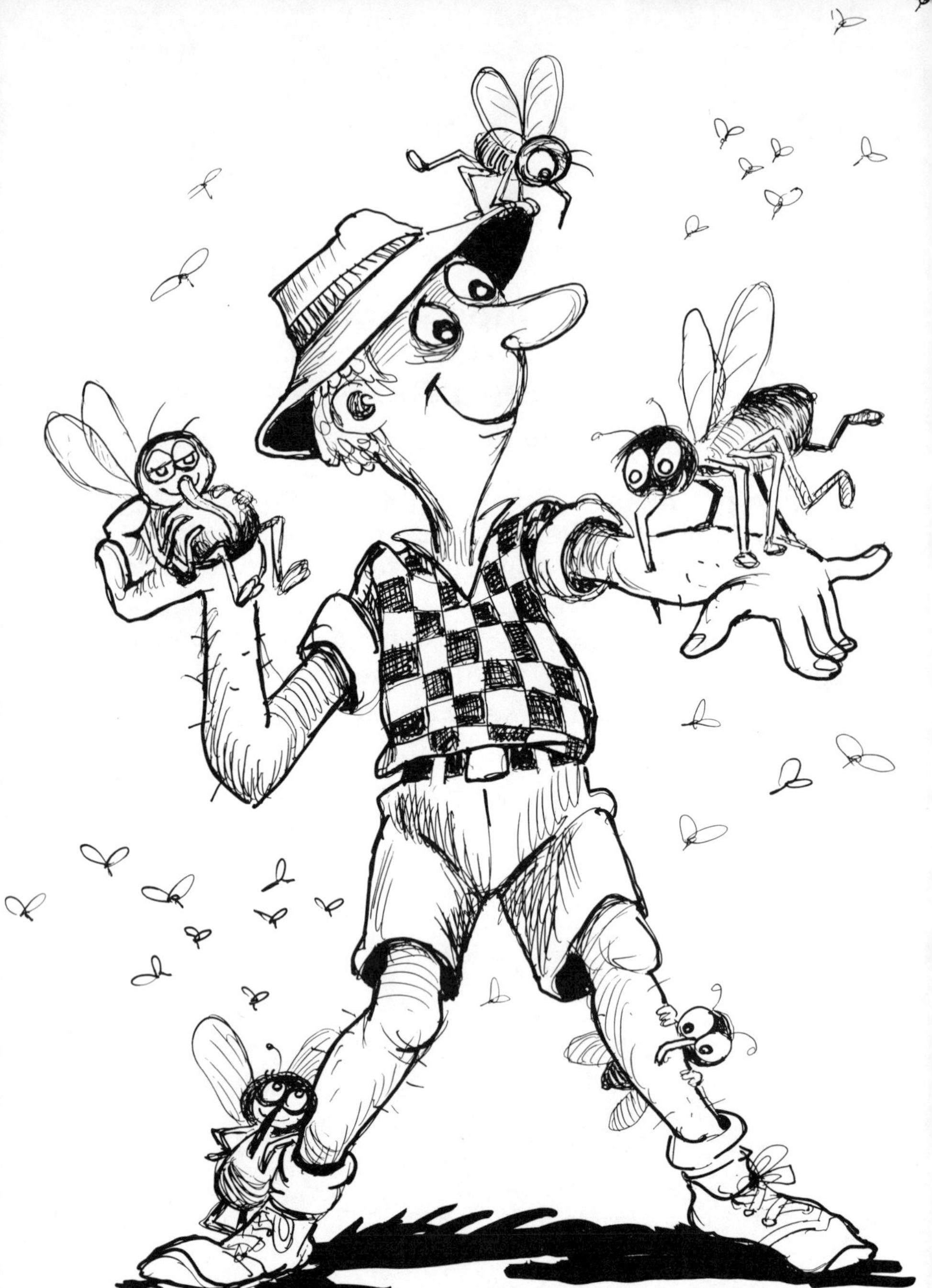

The Mosquito
(216 species, esp. *M. sanguilustus, ferrapenetratum, milliproboscis, persistis and giganticae*)

Brutally slandered — and slaughtered — the Mosquito is considered a Peril only by wimps. As every *real* outdoorsperson knows, the Mosquito presents a classic opportunity for true participatory ecology: Rarely does the layman have a better chance to make a personal contribution to the nurture of Nature's little creations. Investment in a few bottles of flydope to whet their tiny appetites gives the true nature-lover an opportunity to know, understand, and appreciate these friendly, people-loving little harbingers of summer.

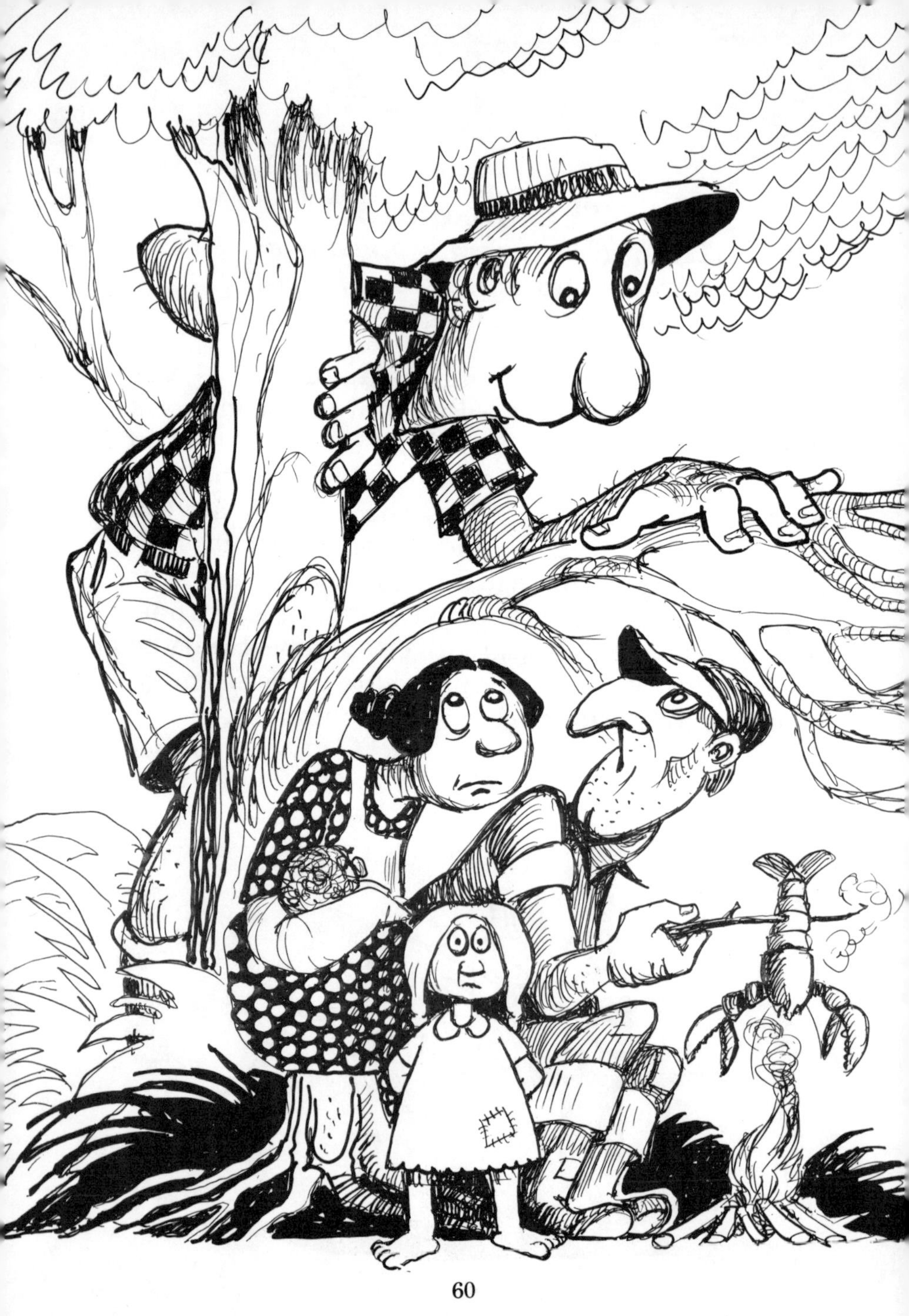

The Native
(Yancae indiginati)

Condemned as a Peril, especially to itself, the Native has been all but eradicated from its natural habitat, huddling now only in widely scattered pockets of resistance. While a few desultory moves — too little and too late — are afoot to conserve the few who are left, breeding as it must only in captivity has made it nearly indistinguishable from its distant cousin, the Fromawayer *(Homo invadium)*.

Please do not disturb.

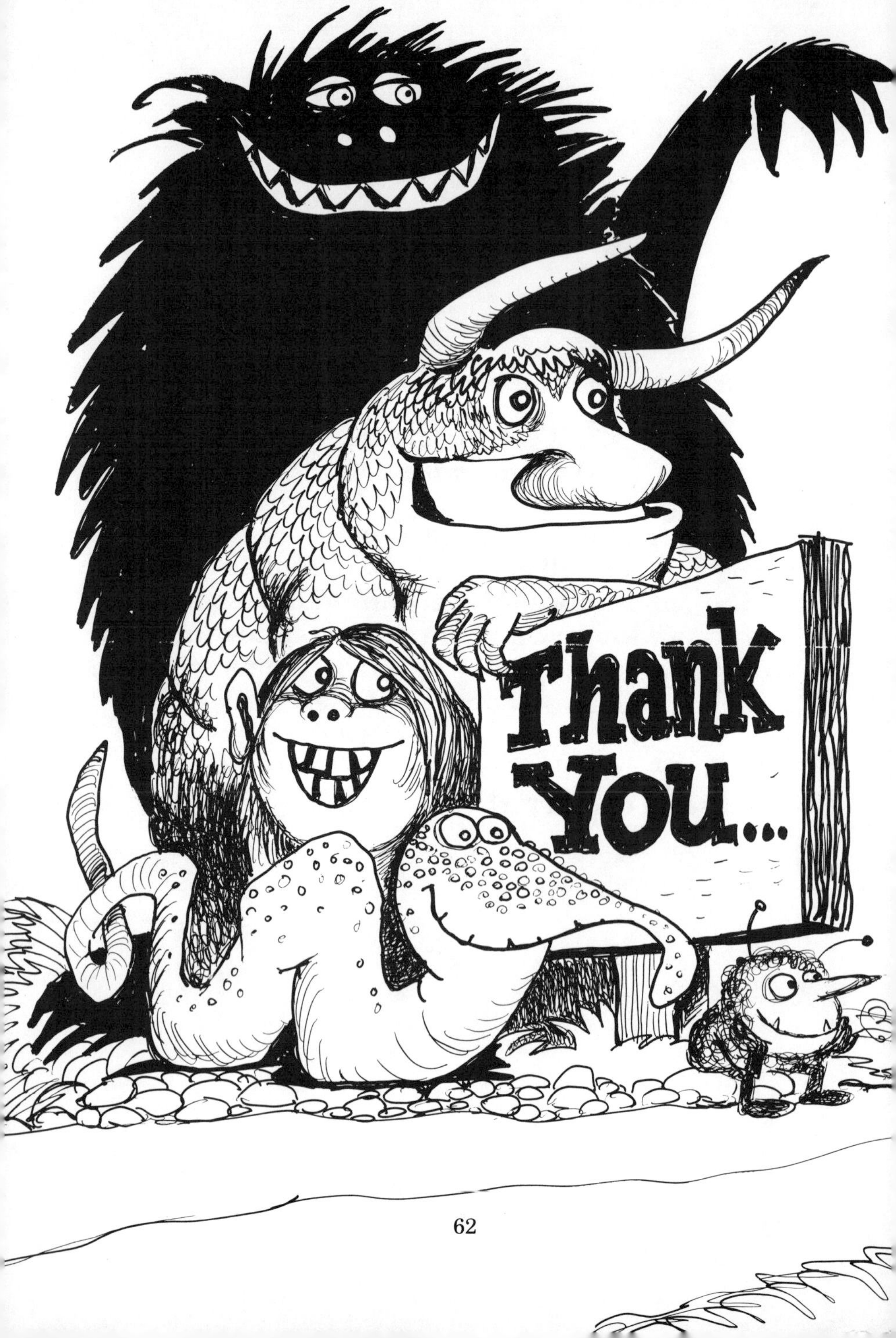
Thank You...

Afterword

A little book such as this cannot hope to cover *all* Perils, of course. The rest you'll discover for yourself — if not this trip, then the next.

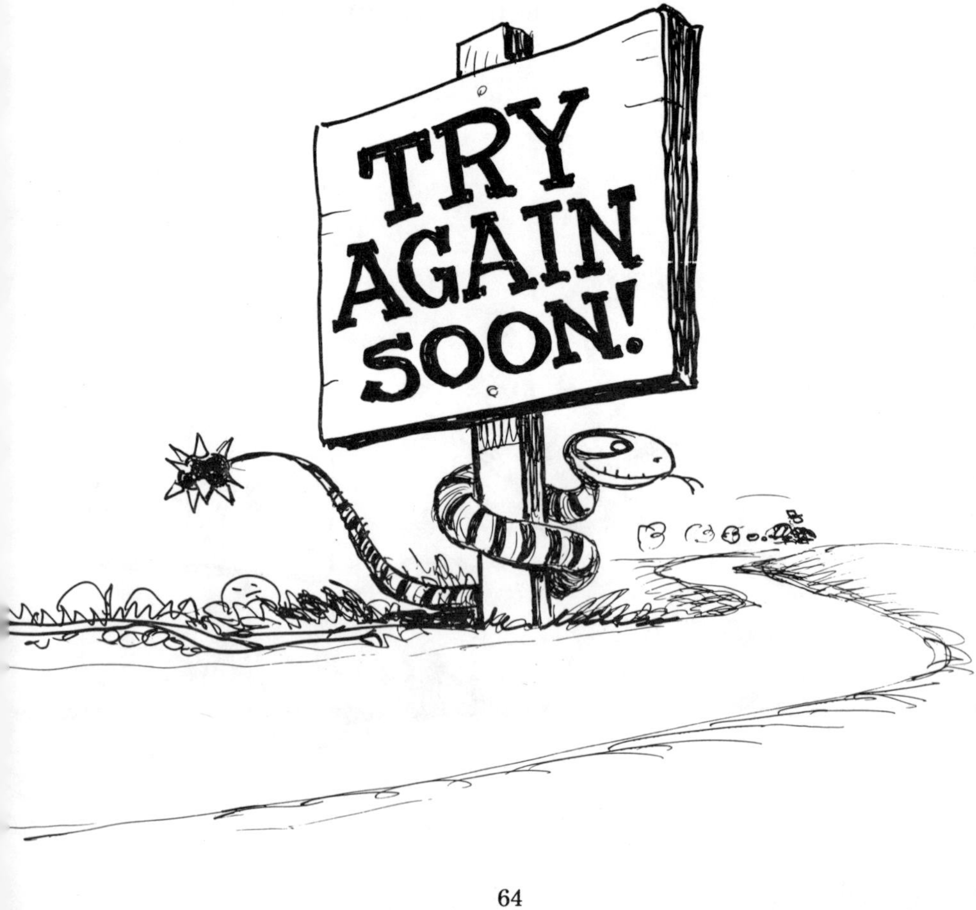
TRY
AGAIN
SOON!